BRIGHT STAIN

BRIGHT STAIN

poems

Francesca Bell

Red Hen Press | *Pasadena, CA*

Book design by Mark E. Cull

Library of Congress Cataloging-in-Publication Data

Names: Bell, Francesca, 1967– author.
Title: Bright stain : poems / Francesca Bell.
Description: First edition. | Pasadena, CA : Red Hen Press, [2019]
Identifiers: LCCN 2018039363 | ISBN 9781597098618 (tradepaper)
Classification: LCC PS3602.E4528 A6 2019 | DDC 811/.6—dc23
LC record available at https://lccn.loc.gov/2018039363

The National Endowment for the Arts, the Los Angeles County Arts Com-
mission, the Ahmanson Foundation, the Dwight Stuart Youth Fund, the Max
Factor Family Foundation, the Pasadena Tournament of Roses Foundation,
the Pasadena Arts & Culture Commission and the City of Pasadena Cultural
Affairs Division, the City of Los Angeles Department of Cultural Affairs, the
Audrey & Sydney Irmas Charitable Foundation, the Kinder Morgan Founda-
tion, the Allergan Foundation, and the Riordan Foundation partially support
Red Hen Press.

First Edition
Published by Red Hen Press
www.redhen.org

Acknowledgments

Grateful acknowledgment is made to the editors of the following publications where these poems first appeared, sometimes in different versions:

Afrikana.ng, "Benediction"; *B O D Y*, "And Then," "I, Too," "Letter to the Man Who Said I Stayed on His Brain Like a Hit of Acid That Wouldn't Kick In," "Revision," "What Rises, Scalding"; *Antologia di poesia femminile americana contemporanea*, "Prayer"; Bared: Contemporary Poetry and Art on Bras and Breasts, "Gift"; *burntdistrict*, "In Which Mary Advises You to Have the Abortion," "Pretty Boys," "Things I'd Prefer to Forget," "You Can Call Me *Ma'am*"; *Catamaran*, "Want"; *Connotation Press*, "Construction Workers Called Police When They Realized A Lifeless Dummy Was Actually A Real Woman," "Definitions," "Taking Up Serpents," "The Bones' Antidote"; *Crab Creek Review*, "Souvenir"; *Cultural Weekly*, "The Yearning to Be Supple," "With a Little Education"; *ELLE*, "In Plain Sight"; *Flycatcher*, "Besos"; *Folie à Quatre*, "The After Sorrow"; *Gargoyle*, "In Due Season"; *Georgetown Review*, "As If God"; *Jung Journal: Culture & Psyche*, "Subjugating My DNA"; *MARGIE*, "The Yearning to Be Supple"; *Menacing Hedge*, "In Which I Imagine George Washington Considering His False Teeth," "The Curator," "Your Hands, Instruments of God"; *New Ohio Review*, "For My 1st Ex-Lover to Die"; *North American Review*, "Woman Singing in Church"; *PANK*, "In Persona Christi," "My Body Broken for You," "Outings," "Sacraments," "Stigmata"; *Phantom Limb*, "If Crazy Is a Destination, You Are My Driver"; *Pirene's Fountain*, "Across God's Table"; *Poet Lore*, "Remembering the Girl"; *Poetry Northwest*, "Prayer"; *Prairie Schooner*, "Cage of Longing"; *Rattle*, "First Responders," "Narrow Openings," "When I Think About Cats," "With a Little Education"; *River Styx*, "Committee Work," "Sending Underwear to Prison," "Severance," "Too Many Men, Each One Leaving"; *Salamander*, "Nothing Dramatic Now"; *Spillway*, "Dreaming Helen Keller," "Heloderma Horridum Horridum," "Just Born"; *Spoon River Poetry Review*, "In the Rush Creek Open Space Preserve"; *Tar River Poetry*, "Belated," "Misconceptions"; *The Adroit Journal*, "Gift"; *The Rumpus*, "Every Two Hours, the Letdown Burns," "Rules of Engagement"; *The Sand Hill Review*, "Getting Away"; *Verdad*, "Flailing/Not Flailing"; *This Is Poetry: Poets of the West*, "Narrow Openings," "Severance"; *This Is Poetry: Women of the Small Press*, "You Can Call Me *Ma'am*"; *Willow Springs*, "On the Way to Chevron, My Father Tries to Save My Life"; and *Zone 3*, "Field Trips."

Poems may thrive in isolation, but poets not so much. I offer my immense gratitude to the following people without whom this book would likely not exist:

My first teacher, Anne Pitkin, who set me on the writers' path with her fine example to guide me.

'Lyn Follett and Susan Terris who are beloved mothers and mentors and friends to me and to so many.

David St. John, beautiful poet and generous teacher, who granted this housewife permission to believe she could be a poet. No matter how long it took her. No matter how many children she had.

Ellen Bass, kind and wise teacher, generous force for good in this world.

Tim Green, Richard Newman, Liz Kay, Jen Lambert, Chris Crawford, Joshua Mensch, and Jan Zikmund, intrepid editors who've given so much of my work its home.

April Ossmann, editor and friend, who conjured a book from a messy pile of poems, polished it, cheered it, and showed me how to send it into the world.

Marta Ferguson at Wordhound who first taught me to submit to magazines.

Everyone at Red Hen Press, for their sharp-eyed editing, gorgeous design work, and robust promotional support. Thank you for not letting me get out the door with food caught in my teeth.

Kate Gale, wicked smart, big-hearted editor and writer. Thank you for devoting your one life to literature. Thank you for giving my book—and a multitude of others—a chance.

My partners in poetry and life: Kelly Cressio-Moeller, Alexis Rhone Fancher, Molly Fisk, Jennifer Hahn, Christina Hutchins, Gregory Mahrer, Tiffany Midge, and Connie Post. You've given me advice, sympathy, love, and editorial suggestions. You've listened to me whinge and swear and cry. No words of thanks will ever suffice.

Barbara Ristine Howard, without whom I would have long ago given up. For twenty-six years of friendship. Twenty-six years of belief that I am, in fact, a poet. For submitting my poems. For tallying my rejections. For thinking I would get somewhere despite all evidence to the contrary. I can never adequately thank you.

My family of origin who have long suffered the mortifications of having a confessional poet as a daughter and a sister. Thank you for accepting me and loving me as I am.

The three humans I'm privileged to call my children. Raising you is my life's best, highest purpose and its grandest adventure.

And Patrick, my dearest, my partner in joy and in sorrow. Thank you for fearlessly loving me.

*in memory of Mabel Alice Grounds, beloved grandmother
and truest friend, with gratitude for her kind heart, her grit,
and the sharp tongue she passed on to me*

Contents

I

II

III

IV

I

As If God

Little mouse, lying white on your side
like a child in a christening dress—

I've thawed and placed you to wait
on the flat, rock altar, but snake

isn't interested. He sniffs once,
tongue flickering like flame,

then slides back into the shavings,
concealed again. It's as if we prayed

and God did not come. Or came, but turned
His face away, refusing to take the child's

whole spirit deep into His devouring shape
and free it. As each mouse released

by generous jaw and steady squeeze is freed
into the great, gliding goodness of snake.

Gift

I used to watch him
from my bedroom window
in the brightness of his den.
Always at night, with my light off,
so he didn't see me gawking
when he removed his white turban,
exposed the coil of hair he never cut.
He unwound it tenderly,
a gift from God.

My neighbor was highborn
and could not mow a lawn
or run a dishwasher. As a child,
he rode a red wagon downhill,
sat as his servant pulled him
back up. My parents taught me
how to work, but reverence
I learned from him.

How to uncover my blessings
by candlelight, house silent
as God, peel away with care
my stiff jeans, blouse with many buttons,
panties a pure, blazing white.
I lingered over my brassiere,
its unclasping a relief like prayer,
let it slowly loose
my breasts, those miracles
risen finally on my waiting chest.

In Plain Sight

By fourteen, I had transformed,
body gone from tight-fisted to extravagant.

The boys, too, had changed. Their voices creaked like screen doors,
then slammed into tones of full-grown men.

They called from car windows and sidewalks,
Big-breasted woman, I love you!

One I liked brought a friend to my door who chortled,
You're right. Her teeth are terrible, but her tits are fantastic.

No blouse would button over my excess.
Nothing in the lingerie department could contain me.

The special-order minimizer cost me fifty babysitting hours
and was unyielding as a harness. I believe in brazenness,

but no power was ever greater than feeling the tremble
in a surprised boy's fingers after I removed that bra.

Oh, my God, one said. *I had no idea.*

Dreaming Helen Keller

Always the interminable spelling
      on my inadequate palm.

One letter at a time, like a slow drip
      off the eaves after a big rain,

and me, still parched, tipping my face
      to the sky, wanting to holler.

If only I could learn to shape air
      into something recognizable.

If only someone would whisper poems
      along the insides of my arms,

a hymn sung by fingertips
      across my belly, all the way

to the peak of each breast,
      my body's rafters reverberating.

Then, a suspenseful little story
      unfolding up and down my thighs,

and finally, a cacophony,
      both lyrical and guttural:

let my little cave echo, trill, open
      like a throat to answer. O, fill my body—

this clumsy, mute organ—with song!

Across God's Table

I haven't stopped loving you,
      man doing time for murder—
            one year for each of the sixteen times

your knife rent another man's flesh.
      Hard time that won't restart
            the delicate engine of his life.

Tattoos cover the body you've built here,
      armor you harden into every day.
            Your eyes are guarded,

face worn out by the penitentiary—
      but we sat across the table as children,
            good food sticking in my throat

when your father thrust his fingers
      into your Afro, jerking us all to attention.
            Sometimes in summer they let you out

of your room to play. I chased but never
      caught you, your body a dark streak
            crossing the lawn. Now, on trips outside,

chains hang from legs you've made
      strong enough to hold what you carry.
            I look at your grown man's face,

eyes shining darkly at me, and the boy grins back.
      Catch me catch me if you can—
            but I was a skinny white girl, never that fast.

Just Born

After painful adolescence,
my looks came in
the way a new tooth breaks
through a child's gum
and shocks everyone.

Suddenly, I found
the world's doors
flung open to me.
My stubborn phone
began to ring.

Sweet then,
the little moans
men made
when I left
or stayed. Sweet,

their helplessness—
like just-born mammals
seeking a teat.
I was intoxicated
by that need.

At nineteen,
I found beauty
waiting for me,
a fast car parked
on a lonely street.

With a Little Education

This is what became of the homely high school boy
with the fine hands and big brain: he ended up sliding
his fingers all day into the vaginas of other men's wives.
Expensive women who book six months ahead
to take off their clothes for him. He keeps them
waiting under a harsh light and thin sheet
before delivering their silver-spoon babies and bad news,
before roving his skilled hands over all the cheerful flesh
once so firmly out of his reach. They send him flowers,
page him after hours, confiding
when their sex lives are painful or dry up entirely.
He coaches them to remind their deal-making,
deposition-taking husbands of the grave
importance of foreplay. He touches their sleeves
as they leave with what could only be mistaken
for tenderness, and smiles, knowing they wonder
what he does with his hands at night. How different
his landscape looks now: his stool a rolling throne,
the world he has mastered spread glorious before him.
If only he had known, when he was pimpled
and pained, that even the hearts of the beautiful burn
in the third trimester, that age bursts in,
without mercy, on everyone, even those girls
as effervescent and confusing as champagne.
If only he'd known how easy it would be,
with a little education, to wake each morning
to a string of women, naked in his offices,
ready for him.

Severance

I'm one of those men,
he told me with a crooked
little smile, reaching gingerly
across the space between us.
Men you read about
in history books, he said,
as his right hand, the hand
with one finger gone AWOL,
vanished into the darkness
up my skirt and crept beyond
my underwear's flimsy barrier.
It was twenty years ago. I was nineteen,
like you are now. I nodded
and pressed firmly against his touch
trying to figure
which part of him I felt—
whether it was a finger he still had
or the one he'd lost
that slipped inside me.

When I got back,
I didn't tell anyone.
Just smoked opium in some hotel,
bought myself a fur coat.
I felt like goddamn Jim Morrison.
I felt like—he paused, shifting
to where he could reach me
better—like what I was.
A man who killed women and children,
fucking infants.
He halted there, to see that he had me

at attention—*I killed with pleasure*
whatever I could. I cried out
at that, but was by then
too far to pull back,
and shuddered helplessly
against his maimed hand,
sure what I felt
was the part of him
gone missing.

Sending Underwear to Prison

Rocking the bawling reminder
of another night's work,
your mother didn't consider
whether cloth or disposable was better
or think while you cried
that baby wipes might be drying.
She worried instead that her pimp
would pull the trigger
when he put his gun to your wailing
head ordering, *Shut this child up*
or I'll do it for you, which caused her
to wonder if liquor or heroin
could calm a baby quicker—
and when nothing worked,
hand you over to the state.

To get at your rage,
to strip away your smiling,
understand why you killed
a man for touching you
between the legs, you have to go back
to that baby, the whole world
chafing you like a cilice. When I shop
for your clothes, I choose your underthings
carefully, reaching to check
how they feel from the inside.
I only send the softest underwear to prison.
I want to teach you tenderness
the way a baby learns it,
through the skin.

Woman Singing in Church

She is not beautiful—
slightly awkward, slightly heavy,
somewhat made-up—
but when she releases her voice,
a fierce, wild thing,
we are pummeled by it, laid open
on the blade of its loveliness.

She seems also to suffer,
as if her voice is an affliction
she can't escape. Singing,
she has the look of a laboring woman
who grimaces as the miracle
tears through her—gazing
toward Heaven as if to see

who put this writhing, keening
song in her. Her face shines,
like Christ's face on the cross,
anguished and enraptured,
as His life poured out of Him in a rush,
the gleaming life
His body could not contain.

Taking Up Serpents

Sometimes my father sends me to the room
where he keeps the church snakes. He knows I'm afraid.
I don't set a foot in till the lights come up bright.

Once a snake got loose and had to be caught.
It coiled in the middle of the room, shocking

as when I broke free of puberty.

Snakes have no ears, but they feel you coming from way off.
Before I get a hand at the knob, they're ready,
rattles rasping. Hairs rise up all along my skin.
It's what happens when boys look at me now.

New tongues speak in my body.

Sometimes I writhe, a belly-crawler, a tree branch grown
crooked. My father doesn't look right at me anymore.

Not since the Devil slithered into me and set up shop.

Snakes, he looks in the eye, holding
each scaled body high, with both hands.
Whenever one strikes him, prayers fly.

I've heard venom makes your heart race,
splits your skin wide.

Misconceptions

The Bible is wrong
about serpents.

God's favor is clear
in the skin

shed in one piece,
the snake emerging,

vivid as a woman
who slips from

the stockings between
her and pleasure.

Notice the jaw: it unclasps
to accommodate

appetite. The sleek skull
is earless. The world's music

plays along the finely
tuned underside.

Revision

Each month comes the reminder
of the gash God made in me.
I like to think He made it
with one finger, the way an artist
will reach right into a painting
and finish it off. Not bothering
with brush or sponge,
just making with a finger
that last mark needed
to disturb the image enough
that the eye believes it.

Remembering the Girl

He would always remember
how blood came from her body

clinging to his cock like paint.
Her cries, he could forget.

These he had stopped anyway,
sealing her mouth with his hand,

pressure to a wound.
Her pleading eyes left

no mark or memory on him.
Only her blood arrested him

mid-thrust, fresh and bright
as poppies. Only this

made him suck his breath in
as young girls do

the first time. Years after,
the sight of his first child's head

recalled the head of his cock,
slick with blood,

forcing its way along.

Benediction

He doesn't want to relive
     what he did to get in here,
freedom sure to come
     only with a rough sheet
pulled over his face.
     He keeps busy as he can,
works for one dollar a day
     in the prison factory,
piecing together mattresses
     for college dorm rooms.
He blesses each narrow bed,
     thinks of first times
away from home.
     Of home. Of new bodies
cushioned by the labor
     of his hands, stretched there
and yearning. May there be
     ample room for them.
May each loss leave
     only the bright stain
of a new beginning.

Narrow Openings

A constant dripping on a day of steady rain
and a contentious woman are alike.
            —Proverbs 27:15

It's hot. The clouds' soft faces
are closed, billowing refusal.
I want to quarrel
with my lover, who sits,
risen dull from our damp bed.
Hair hangs, humid and tangled,
on my neck, but he won't unlatch
the window, doesn't like the noise.
I don't like him very much.
I want to argue until anger splits me
like the flowers on my short dress.
I choose lipstick to startle him, Ultra Violent.
He watches, his hair still holding
the shape of my hands.
Raising my legs,
I let the mirror catch me,
throw him bare skin glistening
sweat. *Going for a walk*, I say,
slipping into the narrow openings
of sandals, smiling as anger reddens
his dim face. Down each block,
I think of him pacing
the closed rooms, stupid and lovely.
Face glowing, I am an August peach.
My feet slapping the sidewalk
a dance as good, as constant, as rain.

Getting Away

That fall, we pitched
a tent in Montana bear country
for two weeks.

Every night, whether we made love
or not, you slipped your rifle
between our bodies.

I dreamed of bear paws—awkward
as children's hands, innocent-looking
as they swiped open my skull—

and woke, face pressed to the gun's
steel snout, warm as our skin
by morning.

You were sober mostly that trip,
didn't even stagger as you hoisted
our cooler up a tree to safety.

But I had already seen you
reeking and fiery enough to fracture
furniture with just your hands

or to crater the walls
with the pointed toes
of your best boots.

I had held you when booze
was a sudden blow
to your head

and you fell asleep mid-sob,
your hard body gone
flaccid in my arms.

Afternoons in Montana,
you fished downstream a ways,
while I lay naked on a flat boulder

in the middle of the river.
On all sides poured water:
a constant, diminishing caress.

II

Pretty Boys

If I were a blackbird, I would fly
sensibly over the stinking marsh
         and spiked cattails, their tops fizzing white—

quiet in my dun cloak.
Lofting after me, the males' songs
         would rise note by note.

I would not answer their calls.
I see those pretty boys as they are:
         swaying in every breeze, clinging

to their hollow reeds. The industrious
easily collect two or more like me,
         and the confinement of the nest

drains warmth from the female body
while the males flit cheerfully,
         beating their beautiful wings.

On their shoulders is a warning
I can recognize: twin lights ablaze
         before the shock of the obliterating train.

Definitions

Am I not your receptacle,
vacancy on two legs,
opening in the front
you pour yourself into?
You leave me with child
who will leave me
with nothing
but biology's bit
stuffed into my mouth,
body split like a lip
and gaping.

In Which Mary Advises You to Have the Abortion

In the beginning,
every last one of them
overshadows like a god.
Their flesh, with its insistent power
of resurrection, rends easily
your inadequate membrane,
silly shroud that surrenders
as destiny is foisted upon you.

A woman's door is always ajar.

A child makes itself at home,
swelling you, as death does
the body, leaving it belching
and bloated. *Be it not unto me,*
you'll beg, *to drag this weight
through the marketplace,
made to love what excruciates.*
Undo the indelible.
Speak your belated *No*
to the great god—
His rigidity, His swarming,
innumerable spermatozoa.

Subjugating My DNA

Sunday mornings, I keep my hands
clasped as the community chalice
goes past. I allow myself
the fullest, individual glass:

a thimble against a ravening thirst.
What's worst is wanting to believe
it's Christ I come for—
though my blood is warm

as the dark, staining curse
my grandmother pissed
in the chair where my father
once rocked me—and wild

as the drunken heat blazing
on each cheek as my great-aunt
screwed on some guy's backseat
parked in daylight on my mother's

street. Her round, writhing bottom
rising now in hindsight's view
brings more to mind
a maggot than a moon.

Lord, I am not parched for You.

The Curator

Jeffrey Dahmer, unable to conform
his conduct to the requirements of law,
killed seventeen men and dismembered them.
Sometimes, he dissolved the pared flesh
in acid and flushed it down the toilet.

Other times, he ate the hearts
and livers, biceps, a portion
of meaty thigh. The bones
he pulverized and scattered,
or soaked in bleach to keep.

When police searched his apartment,
they said it was less crime scene
than museum installation: two skeletons,
a scalp, and seven skulls, one man's head
and genitalia preserved in acetone.

In prison, he asked if forgiveness
was even possible for him.
The chaplain didn't hesitate.
The Lord, he told him, makes no exceptions.
Jeffrey Dahmer did not resist

while the inmate with the metal bar
bludgeoned him to death. He waited, patient
on the prison's bathroom floor, for God
who gathers our shards, every splintered
fragment, into His boundless hands.

Committee Work

The football players,
    when accused of raping
the drunk girl, said *she*
    had approached *them*,
pulled their pants down
    and sucked their penises
into her mouth.
    One claimed he was unable
to achieve an erection
    despite her efforts.
Another felt *inappropriate*,
    zipped up, and walked out.
One was seen behind her
    with his pants down,
but none could say
    whose fluids were found
in her vagina
    or her underwear or her ass.
The school had no interest
    in DNA. The committee
closed the case, and
    the football players went on
to an undefeated season,
    trampling team after team.
They ran joyfully,
    faster than the opposition,
faster even than all
    the drunk girls who rush
to their knees, who bend over
    pool tables and couches,

no longer content
       to just *ask* for it,
no, *those* bitches
       reach out to *take* it.

In Which I Imagine George Washington Considering His False Teeth

Sometimes I visit the stables
wearing my best set
and find her.

Milking, maybe,
black hands quick
at the teats.

She kneels
when I approach.
We do not speak.

She is a wild thing,
all dark eyes
and instinct.

I unbutton and she
opens right up.
Turns out

I fit perfectly
in the gap made
in her gums.

She doesn't flinch
when I rest my hand
on her head.

She knows
I will not
hurt her.

While she is busy
at me, I run my tongue
over her teeth

in my mouth. Their hardness,
their unblemished
whiteness.

The Bones' Antidote

Spending time under Paris is not for everyone, but . . .
can provide an antidote to the surplus of beauty that is found above ground.
—Rusha Haljuci, *The New York Times*

What do you know of beauty
or ghoulishness, of the distance
from our individual graveyards
through the winding dark of Paris,
the priests' whispery, secret bodies
carting us in pieces, air cooling
as we descended this underworld of tunnels
and chambers, down stairs hacked
in limestone by human hands?

What surplus of pleasure
to have my long bones lain across
those of others as I longed
in moments of dread to drape myself
across the proximate laps of strangers.
Pile high our femurs and humeri!
Cross my ulna with the radius
of another and place them
where someone's chin would have been
had the cartilage held.

These corridors of bone send back the slap
of summer sandals, little sighs
of separate, stifled sorrows, the sound
air makes as you move apart.
It's true, our arches have collapsed,
tarsals, metatarsals tossed near the back

46

with all that does not stack easily.
Vertebral columns do not rise,
but scatter. Scapulae and ilia
cast their shadowed wings.

We languish in our piles and pity you
the distal alignments of the living.

For My 1st Ex-Lover to Die

I heard this morning my old lover died, and I cannot
say I loved him, though I may have said so at the time,
cannot say he was a good person or lover or anything
other than a man who called me in the small hours,
driving back roads drunk in his Ferrari, when I was
23 and he was 50, who bought me books and a Lalique
clock that's been broken 20 years, who was the dumb-
est smart person I ever knew, crying in his car at 4 in
the morning, wearing a coyote skin coat that reached
to his shoes, and I didn't want his money or his co-
caine or to be his 7th wife, and I've seldom thought of
him except to remember a dark animal crossing his
driveway at night, and the 2 staircases in his grand
house, going up, going down, and how I held him,
deep in my body, and he made a small, sad sound.

Your Hands, Instruments of God

You stalked them on treacherous
streets where they paced
the lit corners like zoo animals
their inadequate enclosures.
From the darkness encircling
like a snare, you emerged,
and took them to river's green edge,
forests' hushed cathedrals.

You filled them—
first, with your sex,
then, with a dread
that swept through
and erased everything,
the way the spirit
of the Almighty cleanses
a new convert.

You liked feeling
the pulse in each throat,
imagining the heart's
wild beating
against the ribs' cage.
You needed both hands
to break the clasp holding
the new life closed.

First Responders

The day I finally gnawed free
from the anchor dragging
its own boat under,
you stopped me in the drive
to set one thing straight:
were I to sleep, even once,
with anyone else,
you would never take me back.

It wasn't hard to arrange that day
and many days after,
all spring and all summer,
and sometimes more than once a day
when I felt like it, to take a man,
pretty much any man, to bed
or the shower or the high-rise
office building floor. Having been,
despite years of accusations
and interrogations,
as steadfast and inert as a corpse,

I began slowly to revive, each man's hands
on me like a paramedic's, feeling
for a pulse, their mouths bent
on resuscitation, their bodies thrusting
against me insistently as a doctor
pushes on a stopped heart
trying to turn it back on,
their strokes powering my leaden arms
struggling from down deep
through murky water

as I fucked my way upward,
one man at a time, and came
bursting, breathless, back to life.

In Due Season

That day, you stood close to her,
woman to woman, all ten fingers
wrapped around her throat,
and wrung life from her like water
from a dishrag, letting her slowly down
the way a mother does a sleepy child
before arranging her, arms out,
and unbuttoning her blouse
to bare her belly: a shining, shifting mass
you touched gently with your knife
before slicing slowly, as a seamstress
with a pair of scissors struggles
to cut the seams just right—
until one body emerged
from the other, and your hands
pulled it tenderly along.

Her blood's smell, then, sharp as metal,
the sac of fluids washing over you,
their scent like seashore,
your hands slippery but steady
around the fierce little life
as you strained to bring it,
a miracle, from death.

Only the cord remained to be severed
before you wiped the residue of that place
from yourself and the child and turned,
taking her gift out the door with you,
its tiny wailing cradled in your arms.

Every Two Hours, the Letdown Burns

By the time I uncover my breast—
t-shirt, bra, nursing pad—

the baby is at full cry,
its wide-open wailing

like a kettle at hard boil,
over-roiling, at scream.

The sound is a pulled trigger,
spraying milk everywhere.

The duvet will sour.
My shirt, stain.

In this circuit, I'm neither detonator
nor what absorbs the charge.

I'm the casing left behind,
the part blown empty.

When I Think About Cats

I think about that Spokane basement,
how the cats went nuts
shitting all over the concrete floor.
I was sent down to clean it.
Some of it came right up, tidy handfuls
of shit, but some was diarrhea
dried hard, so I had to slop puddles
of hot water and bleach
on those spots and wait,
nostrils stinging, for the mess
to soften. That was the year
I turned twelve, when my family's boozy
heritage arrived in burning-tongued
waves on our shores.
So when I see in *The Atlantic*,
these years later, that *T. gondii*,
cat shit parasite, can lodge
in a rat's brain or a person's
and make them crazy,
I flash back to bleach, liquor, vomit,
all the stains that refuse
to budge. I know metaphor lurks
here: how the parasite can live
in rats but has to get back
into the belly of a cat
to reproduce, how it highjacks
the brain's circuits until
rats are *aroused* by cat urine,
find themselves milling around
in the open like women
who walk bad neighborhoods

after dark, and those male rats
lucky enough to get lucky,
infect the rat mamas,
and 60% of their pups are born
yearning for what will kill them.
Still, I find myself wanting bleary men
better passed with my head down.
I don't want to know
who I am in this metaphor—
cat, rat, parasite—and who
the men may be, lined up like bottles
in a liquor store, mesmerizing—
their breathalyzer-blowing kisses,
their bodies straining to enter my body,
their fluids to make it past
the gates at my very center,
my DNA waiting
with its thirst like a hole
and the edge of that hole a cliff
I look down from always,
where my wildness bubbles up
like the fizz of fermentation
or water that's too hot
to hold still.

Too Many Men, Each One Leaving

This one likes me best when I sit astride
him, legs bent so knees push
either side of his hips. I keep my eyes
closed mostly but don't mind that he watches
my body, the grace of each easy collision.
I like to think of twinkling lights,
snow with no steps on it. I like to think
of Mary, chosen by God. Some say

He came to her room and entered her body
like a man, with His celestial penis
and holy seed. I would be Mary riding
the bumpy mule to Bethlehem, swollen,
crying out as the beast lurches over loose stones.
I would that God visited my sleep, lifted
my shame. But I wake alone, twisted in white
sheets, my mornings littered with sin

and confusion. I lean, Mary, like a sapling
in rain, like you. They ask, and I bend
to tenderness, even passion. I lie down,
delicate and rooted as grass. But each one finishes,
as God cast His one, pure shadow over you
and was done. A small heater whispers
through the soil and clutter of my room.
Its warmth rises, rises—and is gone.

The After Sorrow

Sometimes you set fire to my body,
licking like a flame
what it will reduce to ash,

while I shift and moan—
a pile of carefully laid wood
as its base begins to burn.

Wherever you put your hands
is a point of detonation, fingers
pulling tiny triggers again and again,

and you enter me as dynamite
enters a mountain, sliding precisely in
until bliss demolishes us.

After, you soften into sleep
and slide from my body
the way a person on a steep slope

loses the struggle to stop.
Then I see we are rubble, still and separate,
and grief washes over me like pleasure.

III

Guilt Tastes Like Summer

At four, my parents caught me
naked with the neighbor boy the
same day they took me to the new
pool with speakers and lights
installed beneath the water, and I
was afraid to go under so missed
everything, but we stayed until my
skin blistered, and on the way
home passed a little black girl, and
I was overcome wanting to switch
skins with her, to pull her darkness
over me like penance and offer up
my Irish-Norwegian, glow-in-the-
dark privilege, knowing already
her color was a burden I didn't
carry and longing to be freed from
sunburn which was surely a
penalty paid by my kind, as if the
sun recognized badness and tried
all summer to scorch it out of me,
and I peeled and peeled and was
never any different underneath.

If You but Stay

Sally, it would be wrong
to teach you the letters,

though your skin is light
and lovely on your bones,

though we are in Paris
and you could walk—

fourteen and beautiful—away.
I cannot offer

my six languages or marriage
but can instruct you

in what I cultivate in the dark
split rows of Monticello.

All men were created
equal, but you, my child,

were begotten, *made*
as I make hollyhocks to bloom,

straight and blushing,
even in the shade.

My Body Broken for You

After Mass, I bid him kneel before me
in the sacristy as I have knelt
so many times before the sculpted body
of our Lord. He is in his Sunday best,
shoes his mother shined. Wine we shared
left a rose on each cheek.
He closes his eyes in prayer,
his face as open as a question.
I place my blessing hand on his head
and pull aside my vestments.
Oh, I am as firm as my convictions,
hard as the unbeliever's heart.
I turn to flesh in the furnace of his mouth.
His neck is like porcelain as I bend
over him, my body blooming
from his throat's small vase.
I am burning, burning.
I want to bathe him in this cleansing,
hot stream, baptize myself
in the pure flowing drops
of his tears. Look at us.
Look at us before You, Lord.
We are bursting. We are flames.
We are flowers. We are Your holy,
Your broken, faithful children.

Flailing/Not Flailing

I've heard the drowning
are normally silent,
often still.

Some succumb
at home—dry—
hours later.

What do lifeguards
watch for, blinking
back sun, bored?

Children sink
and bob,
sink again.

The pool closes
its clear door
over them.

Who can say
who's failing,
who's having fun,

what face
distress wears
beneath the water?

In Persona Christi

The priest . . . is indeed, "another Christ" . . .
　　　　—Pope Pius XI

Even as he touched me,
I knew
he was the word
made flesh.

We swam, and
I floated naked
beside him,

my little nubbin
rising
from the water.

Weenie on a plate,
he joked.

In bed, he said,

Take and eat.
This is my body,
given for you.

When he came,
he was salty.
Like sea
in my mouth.

The taste he left
was the taste of drowning.

Heloderma Horridum Horridum

At eighteen, my son insists
on free-handling the beaded lizard.
He pats its head, shows me its jowly
venom sacs. The fat face stays shut,
wicked teeth encased. If it bites,
the pain excruciates. Morphine
won't begin to touch it.
My boy runs his bare, still-smooth
fingers up and down the bumpy body,
courting what life inflicts anyway: pain
beyond pharmaceuticals' reach.

Outings

Sometimes, Father Francis took me
                to the movies.
                                Sometimes, to the morgue.

The bodies were laid out in rows,
                like on baking sheets.
                                Their mouths stayed open

the way my mouth stayed open the first time
                he touched me.
                                Some were stiff, the way I stiffened.

Twisted, the way I twisted. His warm lips,
                his tongue.
                                His finger in my little sphincter

as irresistible as death when it comes for you.
                I came for him.
                                My tiny seed in his mouth.

Then he asked my confession, and we drove
                across town to see the dead
                                staring—fixed and forever—at me.

Avicularia Versicolor

It creeps you out
how I love the spider,

her electric green, her lush black;
each articulation of eight legs;

silk she unspools
like secrets.

I swoon for her
whispering gait,

the appraising tap-tap
up the inside of my arm.

Her many, poor-sighted eyes
are nearly useless,

but the world's vibrations
guide her.

Little by little,
she threads her

slipshod tunnel
and hunkers, waiting.

I've made her a glass house
and drop crickets in, one by one.

They live through nearly
their entire consumption,

antennae rotating crazily
as their insides liquefy.

After, I sigh
as she polishes her fangs

on her pedipalps,
exacting as a hygienist.

Besos

At a Sausalito gallery,
Javier reads his poems
of darkness and lost kisses,
besos, he says, explaining
how the literal translation
is *kisses*, but *besos* are different.
I ask what's missing for him in *kisses*,
and he says, *The Spanish*,

making me think of Spanish
conjugation, its preterite tense,
where an action has a clear end,
and the imperfect, where an action
keeps on, like my first kiss
as I lay in the back of a dirty van,
and a boy loosed his tongue
in my mouth, and my tongue,

no longer innocent, leapt
like an animal from its cave,
my lips opening wide,
in snarling contact with *every* bit
of his mouth, discovering nerves
in my tongue were hot-wired
down my body's long center

to those mysterious lips below
clenching and slickening
as we kissed.
He tasted of rum and sweat,

and I tangled my bitten-to-the-quick
fingernails in his dark curls
and held on, as our mouths
swelled and bruised.

I never kissed him again but stood quietly
a few weeks later, as he was beaten
at our bus stop, his sweet, surprised face
kicked by another boy's boot.
A group of us watched as blood seeped
from his nose and mouth.
When he lay, limp and still, we
and that other boy walked away,

and I failed to recognize how a moment
could continue, like the Spanish imperfect,
and what later turned up missing
for me in kisses was not ever
a language, but the taste of rum
lingering like memory
in someone's mouth, and a body,
laid out, unable to resist.

I, Too

Chilly times,
    all of us hunched
        before flickering half-lives

           we clutch in our palms,
        bent to the small light like plants
    bent to frigid, filtering windows.
I, too, finger the cool, slick surfaces,

    slide screens open and open,
        meaning to work, but, easy as a twitch,
          reach the couple and enter
        their bright space with my digital eye
that can find anything. She is so naked.

Even the hair on her privates
    has been removed, as privacy itself
        has been stripped.

        I watch him lick
      where she's been waxed
  to nothing
then turn and spread her
    for the camera.
      I peer into the little darkness
        her flesh holds,

    thinking how a person can't stop herself,
  how the body swells, helpless,
no matter the cold.

Sacraments

It is with devotion
I beat my rod over you,
beat it almost into submission
before prodding the sweet spot
where you soil yourself.
It's a bumpy ride, Child,
but I thrash the demons
out, and deliver you,
frothing and panting, from Hell.

Things I'd Prefer to Forget

How you placed each gun
in my hands like a live thing,
a coiled spring, a promise.

The .45 with its heft and kick,
its full clip I learned
to slide in, then empty.

The sound when you cocked
your shotgun in the house.
It said, *Put up your hands, bitch.*

How I jumped, unable to swim,
into the cold of Bitterroot Lake,
because you wanted me to waterski.

Your photographs where I don't show:
only the rope, the black lake, the spray
of something being dragged.

That you could shoot *anything*—
gophers, songbirds, grouse
you brought home for dinner.

I hated to eat them.
Their tiny breast meat.
Their easy-snap bones.

Snakes you killed as a boy
with your little bow,
standing on their tails to pierce them.

Your hands clasped
around my throat
during love.

All those flowers
you sent
in apology.

Rules of Engagement

On the ride to laser tag,
      our Korean students ask
if it's possible to shoot yourself,
      to end your own game,
which reminds them of the soldier
      back home who ran off with
guns and *ammunition*, two words
      they get exactly right.
The words for mental illness elude them,
      but he had *something*
wrong, they say, *something like ADHD*—
      their all-purpose acronym
for every kind of crazy—and anyway,
      he hid somewhere
high that he seemed to climb to,
      though here the boys'
vocabulary falters, but he
      went up somehow and
then picked off, one by one, those
      soldiers who daily
shoved his ineptitude in his face—
      his plan, all along,
had been to shoot himself next,
      but the guns he stole were all
so long he could not aim
      at himself and pull the trigger, too.
He spent two long days
      alone with the physics of this
dilemma before his parents
      managed to convince him,

by phone, to turn himself in.
  The car is quiet after that
until my daughter asks them,
  Why are you telling us this?
No one answers, and all the way to laser tag,
  I think of the soldier,
imprisoned for life, unable to escape
  the truth: the dead men,
though cruel, had been right
  about him all along.

Construction Workers Called Police When They Realized
a Lifeless Dummy Was Actually a Real Woman

Neighbors took her body, hung there
on the fence, for a Halloween decoration,
said she always *was* running the streets.
This time, he came up behind,
and she caught herself on the chain link
by the sleeve. He struck her till she swelled
beyond recognition, like those inflatable dolls,
the cheap kind. Every blow fills the face in,
a little at a time, but in the end,
they still don't look right.

Stigmata

A single trickle
from where he nailed me
to the sacristy wall,
pushing hard
to get all the way in.

He said he would
teach me mercy.
For three months now,
my wound weeps
in the dark.

IV

In the Rush Creek Open Space Preserve

They arrested a man last Thursday
for baring what should be kept
zippered as a good boy's lips.

His jangled mind on display,

he wandered, gibbering, in just a shirt.
His genitals swayed, not hurting anyone,
but jarring, even frightening some.

I'd like just once to do the same,

to quit my tidy breakdowns
and fall apart big, to run, exposed
and babbling, up along the ridge.

Souvenir

He told me in the backseat of the Camaro
his enlistment bonus bought.
How the plane disgorged him
in the warm night over the island.
How orders are like parachutes:
what you count on
to bring you safely home.
How he followed his
into the jungle, to where a man
bent over a cooking fire,
face soft in that small light
but softer still when my friend
searched him after leaning hard
on his sniper's training to gauge
distance, and windage
and gravity's complicating pull,
and then to open a bullet-sized
door in that stranger's chest.
My shirt was soaked from our crying
by the time he finished
and reached into his coat,
saying, *Look what I brought you:
a grenade from Grenada*—
then closed his eyes and pulled the pin.
For the longest time, as cold seeped
in, he held the striker lever,
and I held him, his breath
in fragments, my hands
slick on his shorn skin.

Field Trips

Walking students across the Golden Gate, I have to herd them, over and over, away from the bike lane, the peril of ordinary objects.

I think of when I was a girl, how my best friend stepped toward me in her basement bedroom, razored palms lifted.

These children laugh and laugh. Bicycles breeze past, raising up our hair, and the rails run like fences, brightly marking a field of air. All the way across, we stop to touch the steel cables that suspend us. They are twisted like ropes, implements that could bind a person to this world or swing her from it.

A taunting circle forms around the one scared boy as they drive him to the side. They want him to spit, as the guide has shown us, straight down to where water churns like worry in the belly's pit. Another boy reaches until one foot is over the top of the railing.

I remember that heavy winter, sleep like a pillow held over my face. Even now, it's hard to be this close to so clear an answer, to the sound the spanned air makes.

At fourteen, pills went down easily, handfuls of aspirin inadequate against pain. They were white and solid, chalky as the outline traced around a body.

I don't like bridges. Or coils of rope. Or foxgloves' bright bells, beauty that grows in shadow.

The group poses, oblivious, near the place I saw a man jump. He turned toward our dead-stopped traffic, his face lit with energized despair. One moment, he was there, his mouth an "O," a strange, stuck aperture. The next, there was only railing. A ledge. The sill of a window left open.

Letter to the Man Who Said I Stayed on His Brain
Like a Hit of Acid That Wouldn't Kick In

I thought of you this morning, our six years of letters,
and the time you kissed me in the Saturday schoolyard.
How we swung from side to side. Together, away.
It was October then, like it is every year, like it is now,
and that kiss tastes like green apples and leaves flaming
in the gathering dark. Days like today, I swear I hear
the small complaint the chains made when we moved apart.

Every morning, I do my five miles, running up over the ridge
and down around the slough. Once, a coyote followed
almost all the way, and I thought of you.

At Whole Foods this noon, the apples were so perfectly green,
my cart so full. I wish I could tell you I am still the person
you thought you knew. Still the girl who likes things broken,
who lives her life along a bright and growing fissure,
who dances best with a man whose limp keeps time.

Six years of letters, and I barely ever saw your face,
but I remember your eyes, October blue,
and the small sigh it was to wait for you.

On LinkedIn, I see you soldiered some again,
and I imagine you running in the Iraq desert dusk.
When we were young, you sent a tiny, Korean flower
from your base, pressed between two slips of paper you left blank.
I dreamt you lost your hands in war then cried
trying to lift a black veil from my face.

More than twenty years now. No more letters come.

Dear Paul, who wrote of bones and broken bottles,
I often wake in night's harrowed middle
and think how what you wished for me is real.
Sweet woman, you wrote, *stay hungry.* I am hungry.
Famished. So barren, I swell, fecund with ruin,
vacancy overflowing me as if I have no bounds.

After dinner, I push my last, late child on the swings
out back. My hands empty, then fill again with her
as the chains whine the long line of falling.

Want

Small wind tonight
and my face pressed
to the flimsy screen.

Owls ghost our hilltop
trees, fledglings
shrilling for food.

They eat their own weight
in rodents every night,
and shriek

although their sibling
was found, consumed.
Under their nest box,

what was left:
wings sheared intact
from the torso, a few bones,

skull with its working beak,
brain devoured,
eye sockets sucked clean.

This is the world I want.
World of hunger.
World of soft breeze and keening.

Lord, let me famish,
devour my body's weight
in summer evening light,

ache for sky
and the trees' outline—
a gaping mouth—

against it. Let me *be*
the dark shape, sharp
against what is bright.

If Crazy Is a Destination, You Are My Driver

As you begin your mad descent,
      I am baggage you wheel
down the dark, steep corridor.

When the first pills unsettle you,
      I am porcelain
you heave into. If your car keys

offend, I am the sanitizer's dispenser
      pumped empty.
When your siblings' voices land, lit matches

in your tinderbox, I am a slammed door
      locked against you.
Pound my hardwood, rattle my knobs

till I chatter. If you bleach all our laundry,
      I wear the fabrics'
blanched faces. When you are hungry,

mine is the emptied pantry, food snatched
      from across the table.
If you grow lonely, I am the back

you follow all winter. When the days' harsh
      machinery agitates,
I am the chair knocked over, sunflower

ripped from the garden. When tears
      overtake you, I am the rag
you snot into. If the house is too quiet,

I am your breath of vowels, your nonsense
            repetitions. Sing me
the Prozac, render each bright milligram.

The Yearning to Be Supple

Hips are the rain gutters of breath,
my yoga teacher says.
Where in the body, I wonder,
are grief's rain gutters?
Which part can I bend
into a sluice, sweating and straining,
to let sorrow slide through?

Make yourself soft,
the teacher says when I struggle.

She's young and can't imagine
I want to be soft the way
a drunk person is soft
when drink has made him oblivious
to what the world can do,
so the world can do nothing.
He can hurl himself head-on
into each inevitable tree and still manage
his jaunty stagger from the scene.

Prayer

When age sidles up,
a final suitor,
let me turn
and take it
without faltering,
the way my body
opens joyfully
to a man. Let me leave
whatever age touches
unaltered
the way I've never
liked to wash
right after a lover.
Better to keep passion's
proof, its scent trails
and bruises, keep the light
on and watch time
have its way with me,
threading silver
through my hair,
leaving a smoky gray
that spreads
between my thighs.
I want to see
my breasts deflate
like sacks
my lovers' hands
have emptied
and laugh
as even laughter
ruins me, crumpling
the surface of my face.

On the Way to Chevron, My Father Tries to Save My Life

He turns to me while I'm driving,
says, *There's something I should tell you.*
Says, *Truth is, I've worried it could happen to you.*
Says, *Women have been burned clear to death.*
Says, *I know it's weird, but I wanted you to know.*
Then he pauses, embarrassed.

In his pause is room enough for me
to think, *holy shit* and *self-immolation.*
To wonder if he senses, after all,
how I verge on combustion.
The smolder I fight to keep
from flaring up and engulfing me daily,
in the laundry room and kitchen,
narrow confinement of the bathroom.
My washer and dryer spinning years of
not done, not done, not done.

Dinners no one likes bubble over
on the stove, and the toilet is bolted
so close to the wall, the only way
to get it clean is on my knees.
Some days, I rest there like a sick person—
head lolling, hair in my face—
and listen while my children trash the house,
glad the mirror cannot find me:
a controlled burn of a woman
where a raging goddamned wildfire might have been.

I stop the car, and he starts again, my father.
Says, *You've got to stay outside while you pump your gas.*

Says, *You sit back down, you're building up static.*
Says, *Spark'll jump right down the gas tank and light you up.*
Says, *Touch something before the nozzle. Discharge your spark.*
Promise me, he says, *you'll do it every time.*

Later, walking room to room to watch my family sleep,
I stand at each bedside in the dark,
not knowing where it's safe to put my hands.

You Can Call Me Ma'am

Having turned forty-two, having menstruated
lo these thirty years, most often
on my hands and knees or curled, drugged
and sobbing, around the hot water bottle.
Having borne three children and been stretch-marked
and bloated beyond recognition. Having pushed
those babies from my womb as each skull crowned
like live coals against my perineum
and lodged for good measure up my ass.
Having bled and sweated and nursed,
breasts rock hard, nipples like paper
doused in lighter fluid and each child's mouth
a struck match. Having pled and dragged
three children to inoculations and speech therapists,
to grocery stores and Jiffy Lube and my gynecologist's office,
to one hundred and eighty school drop-offs,
and three hundred sixty-five whining, shrieking
bedtimes every year. Having brushed, my God,
so many reluctant teeth and forced the good,
green vegetables down and been pissed, shit,
and retched on until now, all are
more or less righted and headed willingly
where they ought to be going.
Having, as I said, turned forty-two,
I don't want you calling me *Miss*,
or acid-washing even one line from my face,
or lopping off the part of my belly
my children made soft. I don't want you lifting
the breasts they pulled down while
they took my good milk or repairing
the scar on my nipple where one

bit down and left a searing infection, a wound
that puckered like a mouth and oozed into my bra
while I nursed through it. I don't even want you
rinsing the new silver from my hair. I like its steel.
I am as sharp as a thistle now
no deer can lop into a nub.
Let me tell you, at forty-two, it is a deep,
delicious pleasure not to be dewy
or fresh as a fucking daisy.

Nothing Dramatic Now

Night after night this waking,
                    suddenly middle-aged
            and barely able
        to drag myself
                to the kitchen,
                        finding it hard to be in night's gulf
        with so much blatant wanting,
                        where bowls nest,
                fragile and void,
                        poised to accommodate hunger's varied dimensions.
            So many receptacles:
                        deep ones,
                    the shallow
                        with their vacancy spread over a broad surface area.
My daily melancholy is nothing
                dramatic now, just a flattening.
                                Like drowning in a wading pool.
                    Nights I spend pacing this room,
        barren and removed as Jupiter's moons,
                    shining the spoons' faces,
                placing each one
                        carefully
            to rest
                    on the others' emptiness.

And Then

the man remembers your body,
remembers to love you again,
flicks you like a switch
waiting, ready
in the room's shadows.
Loneliness rises from each
reclaimed centimeter,
a humiliating eagerness
rushing you like a hound
loosed in woods, your cry
like baying or keening,
months of waiting become sound.
After, the man sleeps, peaceful,
but you are a door he's opened,
a path grown over now beaten
back down. You feel his life,
which will end before yours,
slide slowly away into the dark.

What Rises, Scalding

Red-tailed hawks make two wide wheels beyond my window, just as the doctor
calls with the suspicion I've grown something in my gall bladder.

I want to be the tree the hawks land in. It's old, and puts out leaves each March,
lets them fall in November.

Today, the leaves are chartreuse, frilled. The spirea nearby keeps making its
wreaths of flowers. Brides keep making their promises, setting out in love's flimsy
conveyance, scattering petals.

My doctor's from Slovakia and says the trouble is my *reservoir of bile.*

I imagine a lake, bilious and man-made, filled with what rises, scalding, in my
throat. Here and there, stones make a path across the surface.

I imagine it's possible to reach the other side.

Belated

Thank You for
        the consolation rain
this day of
        the dear one's
death wish, of a
        possible lesion
on my beloved's brain.
        Thank You for this
pouring on the parched
        garden, too late
for shriveled-black
        willows. Life twists,
narrows, its cliff drops,
        sickening, to one side.
I can't help
        but think I'd like to
have already fallen,
        unhanded at last
and feigning
        surprise.

Cage of Longing

I watch through glass
as pythons couple,

their heaviness unspooled.
They stretch, still, for hours.

No ears, they needn't say
the right thing.

No limbs complicate
their joining.

No hands hold on
or let go.

Their tails cross
one over the other.

Their clear eyes
do not close.

Notes

The epigraph of "Narrow Openings" is taken from Proverbs 27:15 (New American Standard version).

The epigraph of "The Bones' Antidote" is from "Q&A: Seeing the Sewers and Catacombs of Paris." Rusha Haljuci, *New York Times*, May 3, 2011.

"If You but Stay" refers to the relationship between Thomas Jefferson and Sally Hemings, thought to have begun in Paris when he was forty-four years old and she was fourteen.

"In Persona Christi" is based on accounts of abuse at the hands of Father James Janssen as reported in the book *Sacrilege: Sexual Abuse in the Catholic Church* by Leon J. Podles (Crossland Press, 2008).

The epigraph of "In Persona Christi" is taken from *On the Catholic Priesthood*, the 1935 Encyclical of Pope Pius XI.

"Outings" is based on accounts of abuse at the hands of Father Francis Bass, who took groups of his victims to visit the Cook County Hospital morgue, as reported in the book *Sacrilege: Sexual Abuse in the Catholic Church* by Leon J. Podles (Crossland Press, 2008).

The title "Construction Workers Called Police When They Realized a Lifeless Dummy Was Actually a Real Woman" is a quote from a news article about the murder of Rebecca Cade. "Murdered Woman Hanging From Fence Mistaken For Halloween Decoration," *LEX18.com*, October 16, 2015.

"Stigmata" is based on accounts of abuse at the hands of Father Arthur F. O'Sullivan as reported in the book *Sacrilege: Sexual Abuse in the Catholic Church* by Leon J. Podles (Crossland Press, 2008).

The phrase "energized despair" in "Field Trips" is attributed to Nadine Kaslow and appears in the essay "Clues in the Cycle of Suicide." David Dobbs, *New York Times*, June 24, 2013.

Biographical Note

FRANCESCA BELL was born in Spokane, Washington into a family with deep, hardscrabble roots in the Northwest. Her maternal great-grandfather, the son of a prostitute and her client, was raised in a brothel. Four of her maternal grandmother's five siblings were born on the Yakama Indian Reservation before the family settled in 1910 on a 160-acre homestead in Plummer, Idaho. On her father's side, the Norwegian Wikum family, when traced 700 years back, was already renowned for its spectacularly heavy drinking. The hard living continued in America where the clan was referred to around Coeur d'Alene, Idaho as "the fighting Wikums."

Bell was raised in Washington and Idaho and settled as an adult in California. She did not complete middle school, high school, or college and holds no degrees. She has worked as a massage therapist, a cleaning lady, a daycare worker, a nanny, a barista, and as a server in the kitchen of a retirement home.

Bell's translations from Arabic and German appear in journals such as *Arc*, *Circumference | Poetry in Translation*, *Massachusetts Review*, *Mid-American Review*, and *Rattle*. She translated, with Noor Nader Al A'bed, the poetry collection *A Love That Hovers Like a Bedeviling Mosquito* (Dar Fadaat, 2017), by Palestinian poet Shatha Abu Hnaish.

Bell's own poems appear widely in magazines such as *B O D Y, ELLE, North American Review*, and *Tar River Poetry*. She won the 2014 Neil Postman Award for Metaphor from *Rattle* and is the former poetry editor of *River Styx*. Also to her credit are three luminous and eccentric children, a half-trained beagle, and some very nice blackberry jam.